FIT MARRIAGE

Exercises to promote growth in your relationship

Copyright © 2023

All rights reserved. No portion of the book may be reproduced or utilized in any form or by any means, electronic or mechanical, including photocopying, recording, or by any other information storage and retrieval system, without permission in writing from the author.

The purpose of this book is to gain experience and make marital assessments of our relationships. We want to put you in a lab that challenges you, works you, and places you in exercises that grow strength in your relationship in every season of life.

Table of Contents

Chapter 1 - Spandex & Stolz 1

Chapter 2 - Walk It Out 5

Chapter 3 - Couch Potato 11

Chapter 4 - Beach Bums For Life 15

Chapter 5 - Competing For Each Other, Not Against Each Other 21

Chapter 6 - Junk In The Trunk 25

Chapter 7 - HIIT Training 29

Chapter 8 - Change Your Diet 33

Chapter 9 - Cooldown Period 37

Chapter 1

Spandex & Stolz

We've all seen the videos on social media of what fitness centers look like on January 1 of any new year! People packed inside, wearing all the gear, ready to get that new body and look. They've certainly purchased everything they need to look the part. As you watch them, you see that their style is amazing yet the majority still come across as being someone who has never touched a weight before in their life! LOL… it's hilarious to watch. I can laugh because it was me for many years! I would spend hundreds of dollars to look like a machine. What I knew I wanted was biceps that looked like mountains and a chest the size of the front of a tank! Every exercise I did was focused on those muscles. The result of this was terrible, as those muscles would get fatigued within days and the rest of my body looked, well, exactly the same. But how was I to know? I knew nothing about correct form, and I didn't know anything about muscle fatigue, slow burn, or negative muscle work. All I knew was that I wanted what those other guys who wore little shirts and spandex shorts had! Total sidenote, fellas… don't wear spandex to the gym. Ain't nobody trying to see all that man, c'mon!

After many failed attempts on my own, I realized I needed help. I needed guidance. I needed someone to come alongside that I could trust to show me how to not just get started, but stick with it and do it the right way. I needed a coach. What I ended up doing was getting with Kirk Stoltz! Man, this dude was a machine. The total package, and I muster up the courage to ask him to train me. His response was one I will never forget. He let out this amazing laugh that he had and said, "You have a long way to go, but if you're committed I'll walk it out with you!" Oh, trust me, anyone that knows me knows that when I'm committed, I am committed! So my journey to get the body I wanted really began. This brother had me sore in places I didn't even know existed. There are about 600 muscles in the human body, and I can assure you that Kirk Stoltz found them all. I remember telling myself daily, "Just stick with it… it's working." I didn't see immediate results, instead it was very gradual, but each time I lifted more weight or I dropped numbers on any of the measuring devices, I was like "LETS GOOOOOO!"

Were there some setbacks? Absolutely. I remember gaining weight before I lost a pound. I almost threw my scale in the trash and went back to working out with zebra cakes and ice cream blizzards! I had to keep telling myself, "This is a process and every step forward won't be easy." I was committed to taking three steps forward, even if along the way I would take a step or two, or even six, backwards.

Dee and I are totally committed to seeing marriages get strengthened every day! Our own marriage story is a crazy one. So many highs, but also some very low lows. Along the way, we learned there were a lot of marriage muscles we needed to build. To allow them to grow, we had to be committed to practicing new exercises in our own relationships. Was it easy to build these marriage muscles? Not at first. In fact, some of them were downright difficult to work on. But looking back now, did we see big results? Was it worth the work, time, effort, and discipline? Absolutely! Now we believe it's our time to work alongside others and help them to build their marriage muscles the way Kirk Stoltz helped me build mine. We want to give you tips for your marriage, which served as great exercises for us. Our prayer is that this content becomes a fitness center for your marriage. I heard it so eloquently said one time, "If we are a gym for relationships, then people may not need the emergency room for their relationship." It clicked for me after hearing this. If we can work alongside relationships, and equip them with very practical steps that can be implemented immediately, then quite possibly you and your spouse will be saved from the heartache and lows Dee and I went through. In nearly three decades together, we have been to the marriage emergency room multiple times. Some trips were avoidable while others were not. That said, we are where we are today because no matter what the situation was, we kept putting in the work daily.

So, you've bought the gear. You have your workout partner. You're now in the "fitness center." If you are ready to have a healthy, stronger marriage then let's get to work!

Chapter 2

Walk It Out

L et's first start by walking.

"Kurt your pace is ridiculous, I'm not walking like that!" Believe me when I tell you that my wife has said this to me time and time again. I worked for a company when I was younger that taught me that walking between an office trailer and a workstation was money. I can still hear them say, "If you are strolling we're losing money." So I since adopted a walking speed that is utterly ridiculous. I remember taking my wife out on a date for a sweet walk in town only to look back after a few minutes and realize she had left me. Well, actually I left her. Not left her as I forgot her; I knew exactly where she was! I left her 50 yards behind me. I was so used to walking this fast that the mere thought of slowing down seemed crazy to me. I remember a few times… or I should probably say more than a few times…thinking to myself, "I haven't seen Dee in a while." There she was, stopped in the middle of wherever we were, just waiting for me to realize I was the only one taking part in a competitive walking event. As she stared at me, I learned very quickly that I was winning a race that no one else was in.

Dee and I now make it a habit to take walks together. By together I mean hand in hand, with plenty of eye contact, and real conversation all along the way. Just like with any exercise we will be sharing the pros and cons as you go into this. We want to prepare you so that as things are thrown your way, it won't be a huge surprise, and you and your partner will be able to continue moving.

There are many benefits you will see from this exercise.

One is that communication is a lot like riding a bike. It is something you used to do a lot before, but have fallen out of practice with. Most of the marriage coaching Dee and I do with Broken For Better focuses on communication. As humans in this day and age, we are moving so fast. Schedules get more and more full. Not only that, bills keep stacking up. Maybe you even have other humans who rely on you to keep them safe and alive. The only time a couple gets to talk is when the day is over. While hopping into bed, someone says, "What's your day like tomorrow?" An answer is given, the lights go out, they roll over, and it all starts over again in the morning. A walk allows you the opportunity to talk. Actually, more than just talk... it allows you to connect. Spill the tea from your day. Share your successes. Ask about how each of you have been handling the stress and tensions of the day. Describe your love for your spouse. But be sure to heed this warning: This isn't the time to dump all of your baggage on them. Or a time to express all the ways they are not measuring up to your expectations. I assure you that these walks won't happen often if that's what they become. Walks need to be a safe place. A place for the man to breathe life into the security and peace she needs. It should be a place for her to breathe honor and respect into areas of his heart where he needs it.

It also provides a space to dream together. Even if the dreams you share are so far out there and nowhere in sight. Somehow, every time Dee and I walk together, Switzerland makes its way into the conversation. My lady loves this place, and tells me about it all the time! I love hearing this, and it also gives me something to drive for. One day, together, we will go there!

Walking hand in hand and listening to her dreams, I get to physically hold her and be close to her while truly listening. No agenda. No premature plans for what will happen "after the walk". It gives us time to be attentive to each other with non-sexual touch.

Now for the partner who has the higher sex drive, bear with me for a moment! When you read "non-sexual touch" as a pro, you probably thought it was a typo. Non-sexual touch is really a thing. I know, it took me a long time to understand this concept as well. Dee used to always say, "I wish there were times you could touch me without us having to have sex." In my mind, I thought, "Uhhhhh why would I do that? Also, aren't you fired up that every time I touch you I'm looking to round every base?" Then I studied up on this crazy concept of non-sexual touch. WOW... rub her back, hold her hand, massage her shoulders, and cuddle with each other with no sex at the end... ARE YOU NUTS?! BLASPHEMY!

But now, holding my wife's hand has truly become one of the single greatest things in my life. The two of us are connected physically. Skin-to-skin as we stroll through life. We are together and we are a team.

Find a sidewalk, find a trail, or find a shopping center; you can walk anywhere together at any time!

The benefits are there for sure, but like any exercise, this one comes with some challenges as well. It has the ability to make you vulnerable. Putting your cell phone down for thirty minutes, focusing only on each other, maybe a real struggle for many. The vulnerability in laying down that device breathes life into your partner. You may not like it and it may seem crazy, but trust me, you both need it, and your spouse deserves it. It will also help you alert. Alert? We keep talking about the pros, but a con when walking neighborhoods can be dogs. The dogs in our neighborhood are for real!

I've been nearly attacked twice. Luckily Dee was there to protect me and we made it out safely. Be on the lookout. Just like in other areas of life, there is always something around the corner trying to ruin your time with your spouse. Stay alert and vigilant in fighting for the safety and health of your marriage.

Ok, we have warmed up so now let's go walk! Take a mile walk. It should take as long as desired.

Here are some helpful conversation prompters: What's the craziest thing that happened today? Tell me about a dream you've always had that has never happened? When we are old and gray, where will we retire to? Bucket list item? If you could be any animal what would it be and why? What are you looking forward to in the next 2 months?

Chapter 3

Couch Potato

Grab the popcorn (or a healthier option if you are really working out) and watch some trash reality tv show. Before you jump all over me about this next one, please understand, I GET IT! All of it is scripted, junk, and makes me want to throw the remote at the television. Now that we have established that, let's breathe a little and take a deeper look at why this garbage is gonna bless your marriage.

Dee has watched The Amazing Race for as long as it has been on. Teams of two, traveling around the globe together. Competing in challenges and contests in all the most desired places in the world to visit. Almost every season they visit between three and six continents. All of the teams trying to see who will end at the final destination first. I remember jumping into it with her at the beginning thinking I need to be on this show. I don't know any languages, I eat only Americanized food, and will not touch most seafood. My ideal spot is the Caribbean somewhere, and I don't have a fascination with mountains or snow. So it's probably fair to say that I'm not the ideal competitor for this show. Despite that, Dee and I would sit there and laugh because 90% of it she is all about. The new country every day, the exotic foods, and the breathtaking views.

To this day, as she watches every new season that comes out, I find myself being increasingly lured in. Not for the same reason she is though. You see, together we watch the show and talk through the whole thing. She is sharing her heart on the trip. These parts of the world she has always wanted to go to that no one even knows about. Her words are, "To see the most gorgeous places on the planet that God has designed." I assure you that every time I'm like, "Yeah but can you actually see these people that are competing?" You see, my attention is always on the people. It's their story. It is why they do what they do. It is the character and integrity under which they operate. I am all about the players!

Survivor is our new show. Eighteen contestants taken to a remote island. There they will spend 39 days. They will compete in games for survival and for rewards. Every couple days another contestant being voted off the island. It drops to the final three contestants. Those three then share why they should be the "sole survivor". The contestants that were vote off then cast the final vote on who will be the winner of a million dollars. Much of our time is spent analyzing the players. I tell you this because as you learn the players you begin to see different parts of your spouse's heart and the things that make them tick. Dee and I have learned things about each other, or even the people we associate with, by watching these crazy people on tv. You learn more about the areas that are soft in your spouse. You for sure learn the things that bristle them. Believe me, it is a type of open communication that is second to none. The laughter, the analyzing every move together, or the discussion about how or why we would do it differently. All of this allows you to tap into parts of you that may otherwise never be covered.

Sure, not every reality show is beneficial. Honestly, some are actually detrimental to the health of your marriage. Then there are some that you are completely wasting time and brain cells by watching. It is a fact that I've watched countless baking and home makeover shows. And if I really think about it, I'm not sure I've gotten much out of them other than confirming that I love desserts and can't afford the home I really want! Even in those shows, sitting there listening to my wife talk about designing things for a home causes me to love her all the more. Hearing her heart talk about the things that are exciting to her forces me to get into a place where they are also exciting for me. Sure, I guess I don't have to do this. I could instead just sit there begrudgingly. I could be willing it to hurry up and end already. I will say it the only way I know how… when you are willing to put in the work that no one else wants to, you will reap the benefits that no one else gets to.

You will quickly see the benefits of this time spent by having conversations. It can be so funny and eye-opening in many areas of the relationship. You also get to hear the heart of your partner. The triggers, the turnoffs, and the truth to deeper feelings. I adore learning the things that Dee loves and also what she doesn't care for in people.

Now, the struggles with this exercise might be unbearable. You will be snuggled on a couch and laughing at other people's expense! But, press into it. Enjoy it.

Conversation prompters to help you with this exercise: Are you for the hero or the villain, and why? Are you more into traveling shows or in-home shows? If money was no object where would we travel and who would we take with us?

Whew… two exercises down already, five more to go!

Chapter 4

Beach Bums For Life

Dee and I are absolutely opposite in so many ways. That being said, we have found some things that we love doing together. Our number one activity is probably going to the beach together. Now, hear me, even beach trips can be two completely different experiences! In fact before we even head to the beach you can tell how different we are. When I get ready I only need three things. I need tanning lotion, a chair, and something to drink. Pretty simple. Just five minutes and I'm ready to walk out the door. Dee on the other hand, now that is a very different story. After she gets started, we usually walk out 30 minutes later with two beach bags full, some sort of fan, a chair that keeps her out of the sand, and an umbrella to block her face from the sun. She will also have three different books to give her options. We will have enough snacks to eat every 1.5 hours as well as to feed a small army. She'll even bring enough sunblock to make sure that everyone on the beach is covered in a timely manner. Lastly, there will always be some sort of dish to collect all the shark teeth she will find!

Even in the preparation we are very different and will therefore have two very different experiences. During the time we spend together, will have conversations and so much laughter. Laughter as we people watch. Sidenote, why is there always the one dude in the leopard print speedo? I mean, I'm about it. Brother, you do you and own the headspace of everyone watching you. I always tell Dee, "One day, I'm doing it!" To which her reply has never changed, "Not with me you're not!" We always have conversations about future and past experiences. Despite the differences in preparation, once there it becomes a time to just sit and discuss what life looks like and what it could look like in the days, months, and years ahead.

Maybe for you and your partner, it isn't the beach. It can be anywhere. It just needs to be someplace where you both like to go together: "YOUR PLACE." The place where the world is left behind as you both move ahead together. You see every one of these moments should have intentionality. They should be seen as investments in your relationship. Sitting at a park, eating at a food court, sitting on a trail, sitting in the mountains, or around a lake, it isn't the where. Only you two can decide that. It takes sacrifice on both sides. We both like it enough, so that it isn't a major sacrifice, but for your own relationship, you both may need to make sacrifices to find that one spot. Potentially you will need to rotate spots each month. Remember, marriage takes work. It takes both partners dying to self. Laying down our own thoughts and desires to see our partner elevated and cherished in the relationship. When both individuals are operating like this a marriage is moving in ways that everyone is happy. Is it work, absolutely. All of us should desire to put in the work in order to see the desired results we are looking for. So where are your spots?

This time spent at your spot should be focussed on discussing the areas of life that are moving too fast. Kids, careers, and your relationship. Finding the spot that brings tranquility and where nothing else matters, allows for the ability to access parts of your heart that are often glossed over. Surroundings make a sanctuary. A sanctuary is defined as a place of refuge or safety. This environment will create space to allow emotions and feelings to be tapped into. Be intentional with the "where." If it's a place where you stay distracted and busy, you will contradict the purpose of the exercise.

Make sure you are in a place to laugh. One of the largest deficits in relationships is partners laughing together. I'm not talking about momentary happiness. Instead, I'm more referring to the deep joy that a couple feels by just doing life with each other as well as walking into the unknown together. There are plenty of reasons and opportunities to experience pain and sadness together. So with that in mind, I highly encourage you to embrace and truly hold dear the moments of joy that you experience together. Long for joy to be in the depths of each of you. Talk about the times you experienced this together. Talk about the things that have tried to steal such moments of joy from you. These are the conversations you need to have as you long for something different.

When done right, you will find that these exercises don't produce too many cons. Honestly, you have nothing to do but talk and spend time together. Doing so is truly putting into practice one of the key ingredients to an amazing marriage. That is sacrificing for your spouse's happiness. Sure, there is also an unhealthy side to this. Never speaking up, always laying down your own dreams, thoughts, desires, and opinions and becoming the martyr in your relationship, is unhealthy as well. However, when this is done properly, as in two individuals serving, loving, and desiring that the other comes before them, it leads to a union of two souls that truly can flourish in the midst of chaos.

Conversation starters for this exercise: Why is this place your spot? If you could go to your ultimate location where would it be? If you could change one thing about your dream spot, what would it be? Would you like to live in a location like this or is it more appealing to only visit every so often?

Chapter 5

Competing For Each Other, Not Against Each Other

There are a few areas in life I could improve in. Losing is one of those areas. Losing to my wife is entirely unacceptable! Unfortunately, it happens more than I would like to admit. Take the time we went target shooting together. It's no secret she wears the name "Dead Eye Dee" because of her uncanny ability to shoot a firearm. It really is impressive how well she can hit targets of all sizes. On this particular day, I was not in the mood to lose to my wife. So after taking my turn and knocking down 12 of 16 targets, Dead Eye Dee stepped up. Unbeknownst to her, I had readjusted the sights, meaning that there was no way she was going to hit a target. Was it a dirty move? Yes, it definitely was. But on this day I was really not in the mood for the usual lip service I get when I lose to her in something. She took her first shot and completely missed the target. My plan had worked perfectly! Pulling her eyes off the sight, she looked down the barrel. She raised her head and said, "I think these sights are off." I laughed and responded so confidently and arrogantly, "Oh, here come the excuses." Then Dead Eye Dee did something that shocked every part of me. She looked down the barrel and said, "These sights are absolutely not right. But it's ok, I just won't use them." Five minutes later, I hung my head in defeat as Dead Eye Dee had knocked down 14 of 16 targets.

Some relationships will fight over this exercise. Relationships can get so competitive that some will even compete on who gets to pick the game. In no way is this exercise intended to create tension and fighting. It is, however, designed to draw out of you what is inside you. Done properly, competition can be extremely beneficial to a relationship. Competition for Dee and I allows us to enjoy some crazy moments together. It allows us to see strengths in each other that are otherwise hidden. It allows one person in the relationship to be commended and uplifted by the other. I have often learned the gifts and strengths of my wife just by watching and analyzing every move she makes when we compete. Learning those things has allowed us to function really well together. There are other times in life when those gifts and that knowledge are needed. Competing also has the ability to bring you closer together intimately. Let's be honest, for every married couple out there, that is never a bad thing!

Now before you dismiss this and tell me that you and your partner are both so competitive that you always fight and can in no way participate in this exercise. I would ask you to push back away from this book and ask yourself why that is? What does competition bring out that creates an environment that is not healthy? Is it insecurity? Possibly an inferiority complex? Does it leave you feeling less worthy? These are all real feelings, but there has to be a reason for them. Are there past hurts and traumas in your life? Are you still trying to be something you have strived to be your whole life? Do you have areas in your mind and heart to deal with on another level? Healthy competition should be fun and energizing for a relationship. In no way should it be a dividing tool between two people who deeply care for each other.

I want to encourage you here, even if this type of exercise has never worked for your relationship. You may have tried multiple times, with it always ending badly. Again, ask why. Deal with the real issues and then try coming back together one more time with nothing more than a builder-type mindset. Believe me: Two people chasing the same thing makes the journey so much easier!

You should start this journey by competing together in something. Solidify the foundation that, despite 'competing', you are ultimately on the same team. This will allow you to compete together and secure victories together in a fun and loving way. Competing against Dee and encouraging and cheering her on, despite defeat, shows the things that I support in her and about her. Many times it is these qualities that are buried and never spoken into. Listen, and take it slow. Keep the main thing the main thing. That is, you are a team. You are for the other one succeeding in life. And when one succeeds, you both succeed.

Chapter 6

Junk In The Trunk

When did you last go to a flea market or swap shop? I love going to the flea market. I love walking booth after booth of complete junk. Most of it is stuff that someone has cleared out of a room in their home and has now decided that they must sell it to some poor soul who will probably end up never doing anything with it. Unfortunately, most of the time, I am that poor soul. Every time I go to the flea market, there seems to be so many things I have wanted my whole life, and this is the day that I finally get to buy them. Now I know it will end up sitting in my garage, and I will likely give it away for 20% of what I paid for it at the next neighborhood garage sale! I love

Denette's response every time and without fail, "Babe, what are you going to do with that?" Then I spend the next 5 minutes selling her on why I need this and how fantastic this item will be when I do whatever I do with it. Then there are those times when she hits an antiques booth. A booth with nothing but old furniture in it. These are the booths that make my wife's eyes light up. For the next 10 minutes, I will hear all about the things she could do and will do with this old piece. She is unbelievably creative and has a fantastic talent for bringing old things back to life. So, I listen. Then I root her on and tell her, "I don't see it, but I have so much faith in you." That's when it happens. The thing that I dread the most. The thing that drives me crazy. After 12 minutes of conversation, I pick up the item to carry it to the register. I am ready to buy this old piece of junk for my bride. Suddenly, I'm then hit with the following words: "You know what? Forget it. We don't need to spend the money on that." NOOOO… we just talked about this for 12 minutes! You have dreamed of what this will be. I used brain space I didn't even know I had, and because this flea market item costs 6 dollars (before negotiations), you now don't want it! What a waste. Sure, the thing I bought is an absolute waste of money, but at least we hunted, and we conquered. To go on a hunt only to let the prey go… WHY?!

The real reason I love these trips with Denette is the communication. I hear her work her creative muscles. She dreams the craziest things. In these moments, I've learned about the things she had as a kid and how those items impacted her. I also learn about moments in her life when something hurt her. We laugh at old Bill, who will spend his entire day at the flea market, while no one ever buys anything he's selling. It costs you nothing but to laugh, converse, and dream. Finding a project to do together is invaluable. Can you find something old for you and your partner to make new again? Working together on this is extremely important. Learning the gifts each of you brings to the table to make something a masterpiece is huge.

Every relationship, at some point, will have moments where things have grown old. These are the times where the relationship isn't moving forward. Creating exercises and habits will help you find ways to make old or even dead things in the relationship come to life again. Refrain from being ok with the status quo. Have the desire to see the gold that is in your partner. Honestly, I still have to work at this as it's not a strength of mine. I am willing to come alongside Denette and learn new things. Just as she can make an old piece of furniture come to life, she has a gift for making this old dog learn new tricks.

Doing so will force you to use tools that you've never used before. It will cause you to look beyond what you see in front of you and move you to see things for what they can be. You will start to believe that you can have a more desired product than you have today. All of the things mentioned here must be operated weekly, if not daily, in every relationship. So why not have fun learning to use these exercises to your benefit instead of being complacent with the old junk that keeps collecting dust daily?

Chapter 7

HIIT Training

The year was 2021. I was in fantastic shape and was getting stronger by the day. I spent a lot of my time at the gym and was drinking protein powder regularly. Not only was I in the zone, but my wife was also going to a workout group three mornings a week. She was doing fantastic. She was getting strong and looking toned. Whenever we talked about her workouts and she tried to explain it to me, I would honestly zone out and all I could picture was her and her friends "prancercising" (if you don't know what that is, check it out on YouTube). I mean how do you get stronger not throwing around weights? I thought,

"Well, it's working, and I'm sure your group looks cute doing these jazzercise-type exercises."

Denette came to me one week and told me her group was doing something special. It was bring your spouse to group week, so she asked me if I would be willing to go with her. I'll never forget committing to my wife that I would go dance around with her on that Friday. She was so excited as she had asked many times before. I got up that day and did my usual daily pre-workout routines. Meanwhile, she woke up on cloud nine as her man was going to work out with her. While I was thinking to myself, "Just go and do this, and then you can go to the gym and actually workout."

We arrived a few minutes early, and it was everything you could imagine it would be. There were nine ladies and me. Strike One. We were immersed in the cutest playlist of Kelly Clarkson and Taylor Swift you have ever heard. Strike Two. I looked around and saw a 78-year-old woman and a mom who couldn't find a babysitter and walked up with a baby strapped to her. Immediately I knew this was a bad idea, and I was looking for a way out.

We started, and I immediately found out what HIIT training means. High-Intensity Interval Training. That means no breaks, running until you can't move, and weighted burpees until your knees hurt. At one point, I looked up, and the 78-year-old woman was lapping me in our exercise! The trainer started yelling at me that I was doing the wrong exercise, so I had to respond that I wasn't as far along into the workout as Ms. Mary. She was owning me, and I couldn't do anything about it because I could no longer find oxygen in the air. Well, I thought that was the worst part… but it wasn't. The nightmare finally ended when I looked behind me and an ole girl with the baby strapped to her was doing two burpees to my one. My pride was totally shattered by the sight of this. I went and found a shirt with sleeves and sat in the car. The moment that little fiery trainer came over and said, "Thank you so much for coming today. I really hope we see you again," I responded without hesitation, "Mam, thank you for today and for showing me something I will never participate in ever again."

I gained a whole new respect and appreciation for the work my wife had been putting in, something I had thought the opposite of before. In the terrible moments, I also realized that all the work I was doing was a completely different muscle group than the work my wife had been putting in. It caused me to reevaluate some of my workouts and add something new to my daily routines. I was able to improve myself through this experience, even when I didn't think the improvement was needed.

Making new memories is a core value of the Schaer family. We believe in new experiences together and building a foundation that continues to strengthen. In creating new memories, you can not rest upon the things you have done in the past. You must learn and work areas of your heart and mind together in ways you've never done before. Finding something you have never done before is easy. The world we live in offers so many excellent opportunities. Some may cost money, while many only cost time. Time is a commodity. You only have so much of it. You can't make more time. There are only 24 hours in a day, so how you invest that time with your partner truly matters.

Dee and I often say no regrets, only memories! Find something that you and your partner can do together. Paint, box, go to a play, go to a museum. Take a day out and have a picnic together. Rent electric bikes. There are so many options available to you. My wife and I spent the other day reviewing a list online, it was titled: 'Bucket list things to Do as a Couple.' We were shocked and fired up when we realized that we had already done so many things on the list. If we can do it, you can do it too. You just have to want it, and you have to be willing to try it!

Chapter 8

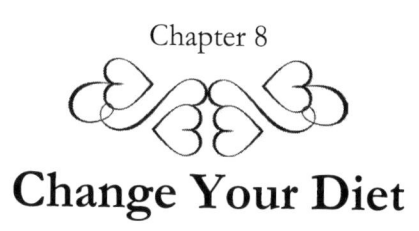

Change Your Diet

Every time I have gone on a fitness kick, I have repeatedly heard one thing. 20% is working out, and 80% is your diet. Like most other men, I focus on the 20% and have never once changed the other 80%. So, needless to say, I don't see the results I desire.

I say it constantly: Behavior modification is easy for a period. But over time it gets exhausting, so you ultimately revert back to the same behaviors you started with. We have written this book to give you easy and proven exercises. We also want to take a moment and challenge you on what you are allowing yourself to consume 80% of the time. So think about this: What are you allowing into your heart and your home that potentially undermines the other 20% of your work?

For behavior modification to stick, and be an easy transition, it has to follow heart transformation. Each of us must be willing to inventory the depths of our hearts and minds to determine if things are coming between ourselves and our spouses. Does social media do this? What about the movies or tv shows you watch? What radio do you listen to? Do the people that you listen to speak life into your relationship? Are they empowering or undermining what you are trying to build? You can do all the right exercises, but if you are consuming things regularly that plant seeds against a life-giving relationship, you will ultimately begin to drop the behaviors and gravitate toward the things that are easier to pallet.

I'll never forget one of the times I was trying to lose weight. I jumped on a fad diet and figured I would do part of what they said and what I knew would work. Their interest was to drop carbs. I only drank water for ten straight days. By doing so, I thought I'd lose a tremendous amount of weight, extremely fast. Day one...headaches. On day two, I was miserable. On day three, I wanted to punch someone. Honestly, days four and five were pretty easy. On day six, I played in an all-day softball tournament in the Florida heat. We were mid-way through the first game when I had to pull myself out. I was hunched over and really not doing well. My behavior was unsustainable and unhealthy. I was starving myself of the things I needed for strength and endurance.

Like the human body, all relationships have elements that are vital to their success. That list may be different depending on who you speak with. For Dee and I, faith, memories, quality time together, and traveling are on our list. These are the things we consume for the health of our relationship. Yours, of course, may be slightly different. And there's no problem with that! All we ask is that there is honesty about what you are consuming daily. Consume things that are nutrients to the growth of your relationship. Find those things that strengthen you at the core. Doing challenging work allows you to see the desired results you are looking for. You and your partner will also begin to love each other in ways that others look at and marvel!

Chapter 9

Cooldown Period

Hear us out here, we are giving workouts after all! You may need to have a slightly altered version of the exercises. You may even need a personal trainer to help in areas you get stuck in.

Have you ever watched old fitness videos? First off, the outfits and the hairstyles are amazing! But that's a different topic for another book. What you will generally see is the lead trainer doing the exercise. Then you will see people to the lead's left and right doing variations of that same exercise. So before you shut this one down, think of a variation of any of these exercises that works for your relationship.

Create disciplines that you stick to each week. Disciplines that you can measure. Do the things that give you results that you and your partner desire to see. The worst thing you can do is overthink it. Enjoy the process. Celebrate the wins. Hold each other during the complex sets. Whatever you do, commit to giving all you have and doing it together!

Kurt and Denette Schaer

Made in the USA
Middletown, DE
29 January 2024